WRITE AFTER

Group Projects as Pre-Writing Activities

Heather McKay
Northern Virginia Community College

Abigail Tom
Githens Middle School, Durham, North Carolina

Alemany Press
Regents/Prentice Hall, Englewood Cliffs, New Jersey 07632

Library of Congress Cataloging-in-Publication Data

McKay, Heather, 1950-
Write after : group projects as pre-writing activities / Heather McKay, Abigail Tom.
p. cm.
ISBN 0-13-042763-2
1. English language--Study and teaching--Foreign speakers. 2. English language--Rhetoric--Study and teaching. 3. Report writing--Study and teaching. I. Tom, Abigail, 1941- . II. Title.
PE1128.A2M387 1993 93-6738
808'.042'07--dc20 CIP

Acquisitions editor: Nancy Baxer
Production supervision, interior design,
and desktop composition: Noël Vreeland Carter
Cover design: Mike Fender
Pre-press buyer: Ray Keating
Manufacturing buyer: Lori Bulwin
Schedulers: Leslie Coward and Ray Keating

To our colleagues and students in St. Louis University, Northern Virginia Community College, Fairfax County Adult Education, Arlington County, and Amphitheater School District, Arizona.

Printed in the United States of America
10 9 8 7 6 5 4 3 2 1

0-13-042763-2

Prentice-Hall International (UK) Limited, *London*
Prentice-Hall of Australia Pty. Limited, *Sydney*
Prentice-Hall of Canada Inc. *Toronto*
Prentice-Hall Hispanoamericana, S.A., *Mexico*
Prentice-Hall of India Private Limited, *New Delhi*
Prentice-Hall of Japan, Inc. *Tokyo*
Simon & Schuster Asia Pte. Ltd., *Singapore*
Editora Prentice-Hall do Brasil, Ltda., *Rio de Janeiro*

Contents

Introduction

Write After is a writing resource book for teachers of intermediate and advanced ESL classes. In writing it, the authors have drawn upon their extensive experience teaching secondary, university, and adult students in the United States and overseas.

All the activities in the book are interactive; that is, they require students to work in groups and to discuss the work they are doing. Through this process students begin to think of writing as a collaborative process between themselves and their audiences. Discussion provides a way to explore, develop, and revise ideas. Students have a chance to try their ideas out on others before putting them down on paper. This is especially important for those who are inexperienced writers. Through discussion, students become more comfortable talking about subject matter in English and have greater investment in the writing that follows.

Because the book combines oral and written activities, it is suitable for use in a separate writing class or as part of a program of integrated skills. This combination also allows for the variety of students ESL teachers deal with. For example, some students feel more comfortable speaking than writing; others prefer writing to speaking. In addition, students come with very different writing histories. Some are accustomed to engaging in academic pursuits and feel frustrated by their inability to express their ideas as elegantly in English as in their first language. Others have done little writing before and may indeed have been actively discouraged from doing so (they were not "ready" to write). Still others have copied the writing of others but have not engaged in the development and expression of their own ideas.

Many students have been taught that writing is a linear process. First a writer decides what to write about and in what order and then writes the essay. But most writers find that it does not work that way. Writers need to explore ideas, try them out, revise them (or perhaps discard them). This book emphasizes that process.

The topics included in this book are: language learning, work, education, cultural awareness, media, and relationships. They have been chosen because they are of general interest. They are all topics about which students have some experience and ideas. Because the topics are familiar, students are encouraged to use previously acquired knowledge about the world and how it works, something that many students do not do automatically but that they should be encouraged to do. The material in the book is intended to stimulate students to think further about these familiar topics and to develop ideas they can write about.

All of the topics have a cross cultural dimension. However, while all of the exercises encourage cross-cultural awareness, very few require direct experience of living in a foreign country. These are identified in the table of contents by an asterisk and may be included or excluded according to the makeup of your class.

Within each topic there are eight activities. It is not assumed, however, that the teacher will complete all of the activities on a given topic with her classes, but that she will choose those that are appropriate and interesting to her particular students. The activities exemplify a variety of techniques, which could be used with other subject matter. Most of them can be done in less than one class period. Each one is complete in itself and requires minimal preparation time.

Each activity is used as the basis for a writing assignment (writing output) to be done in or out of class. The forms of writing output are varied. Students may be asked to report on what they have discovered or to write an opinion. They may be asked to write a letter or a report. They may need to organize their writing to show comparisons and contrasts or to support their opinions. The length and complexity of these assignments can be adjusted to suit the levels of the students. Although two outputs are provided for each activity, it is anticipated that the teacher will choose only one.

I CULTURAL ADAPTATION

1. Cross-Cultural Encounters
2. Letters
3. Word Blitz
4. *Quotations
5. Situations for Discussion
6. *Finish the Sentence
7. Stress and Sickness
8. Whose Problems?

Activity: **Cross-Cultural Encounters**

Task: To experience and explore some cultural differences

Organization: Small groups, half class, whole class

Materials: Copy the *Object Cards* on page 4 onto two different colors of paper. Make enough copies so that each student will have one object of each color. Make copies of Work Sheet A from page 5 for half the students in the class and copies of Work Sheet B for the rest.

Time: 40 minutes

Directions: Divide the class into two groups and designate them Group A and Group B. Separate the groups, using different rooms if possible. Give each student a copy of his group's work sheet to read. When the students have finished reading, give them five minutes to discuss and practice the rules and behaviors indicated on their sheets. If the class is large, Groups A and B may be subdivided for this step. If both groups are in the same room, this discussion and practice should be done in such a way that members of the two groups do not hear and see each other. Next, explain to the class that they will each receive two cards. Designate one color the *Haves* and the other the *Needs*. Hand out the cards in such a way that the Haves of one group match the Needs of the other. The students will then walk around the class and talk to people in order to locate those whose Have cards match their Need card. The teacher may want to demonstrate this part of the activity. In searching for the cards, the students must follow the cultural rules and behaviors they have just read and discussed. Give them five to ten minutes to try to locate the cards. Then send the students back to their original groups. Ask them to discuss how they felt about the people from the other culture and to make a list of the rules that they thought the people from the other culture were following. Finally, have the groups report back to the whole class. Discuss the observations and feelings resulting from the exercise.

Writing Output:

1. Describe your feelings while you were playing the game and explain why you think you felt that way.

2. Compare the two cultures described in the game.

3. Compare your culture and American culture on the issue of touching. Interview one or two Americans to check when they feel they can or can't touch someone.

(This activity owes much to *Bafa Bafa* (1973) R. Gary Shirts, Simile II CA. *Department of the Navy* Contract No. 0600-73-C-0668)

Cross-Cultural-Encounters Object Cards

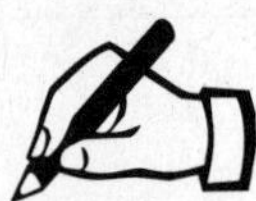

text book	clock	skirt	flower
purse	chalk	television	skillet
lamp	jacket	radio	hammer
tire	ball	gun	mirror
telephone	sweater	chair	rug
bicycle	ruler	blanket	aspirin
pair of scissors	knife	towel	hat
scarf	vase	pizza	jug

Cross-Cultural-Encounters Work Sheets

Work Sheet A

1. Time is very important in your culture. When you are talking to someone you must get to the point quickly. Otherwise, they will think you are wasting their time.

2. In your culture it is important to look directly into the eyes of the people you are talking to. If you do not, the people you are talking to may get the idea that you are not being completely honest with them.

3. When you are talking to someone in a friendly way, you stand close enough to them to feel their breath.

4. In your culture it is impolite to talk about another person's belongings—clothes, furniture, etc.

Work Sheet B

1. Politeness is very important in your culture. When you meet people, you must show an interest in them and their family. This is particularly important if you have a request to make of them, as they must be convinced that you like them for themselves—not for anything they can do for you.

2. In your culture when you are talking to people, it is polite to look down except when you have a problem understanding what they are saying.

3. When you are speaking, you should stand several feet away from the person you are talking to. This is so you will not breathe on them and spread germs.

4. To say *thank you* politely, you put your hands together and bow your head without speaking

Activity: **Letters**

Task: To explore the different stages of culture shock

Organization: Individuals, pairs, groups

Materials: A copy of the outline on page 7 for each student: a complete set of the four letters on pages 8 and 9 for each group of four students

Time: Two class sessions

Directions: Hand out the outline and ask the students to read it. Then discuss it point by point. Encourage the students to share their own experiences. Next, divide the class into groups of four. Give a different letter to each group member. If groups have more than four members, two can share a letter. Each letter illustrates a stage of culture shock as described in the outline. Instruct them to read their letters and then tell the other group members about them. The group as a whole will then decide which stage is represented by each letter.

Regroup the students so that students who read the same letters are together. Ask the groups to use the outline and the letter to write a paragraph about the stage of culture shock that their letter illustrates. Tell them that each student will need a copy of the final paragraph.

Then ask them to return to their original groups. First, have the groups read and edit each paragraph together. Then instruct them to combine the paragraphs into a longer essay. They should try to make transitions between paragraphs. Finally, ask them to write an introduction to the essay.

Writing Output:

1. Think of and write down an incident from your experience that illustrates one of the stages of culture shock. Let other members of your group read it and decide in which stage it belongs.

2. Choose one of the letters and answer it.

Letters: "Stages-of-Culture-Shock" Outline

Stage I:

1. You don't know much about the people and the place.
2. You mainly see the similarities between the new culture and your own.
3. You feel very excited, euphoric.
4. Everybody tries to help you because you are a newcomer.

Stage II:

1. You begin to see a lot of differences between the new culture and your own.
2. You feel that the people of the host country are not very friendly toward you and you begin to feel negative toward them.
3. Everything seems more difficult than you thought it would be. You begin to wonder if you'll ever be able to fit in.
4. You lose your sense of humor and sometimes small irritations seem a lot more important than they really are.
5. You enjoy spending time with fellow countrymen complaining about the host country.
6. You feel homesick.
7. Your eating and sleeping patterns change and you may experience stomach upsets.

Stage III:

1. You gradually increase your understanding of the language, the culture, and the people.
2. You gradually accept other ways of living and thinking.
3. You get back your sense of humor and stop exaggerating minor problems.
4. You become more confident and feel you know more about yourself and the host country.

Stage IV:

1. You feel able to understand the local culture.
2. You are more able to deal with any difficulties that arise.
3. You enjoy exposure to the new culture and experiences.

Letters for "Stages of Culture Shock"

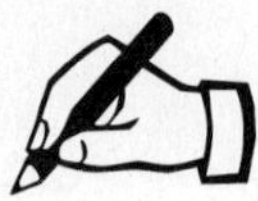

Letter 1

Dear Mother,

I often wonder if I'll ever be able to live in our country again. The way of life here has become natural to me. I was thinking about that the other day when I was on my way to a meeting and I ran into a friend. Of course, I stopped and talked for a few minutes. It would be rude not to. And I didn't even look at my watch the way I would at home. I got to my meeting a little late, but nobody seemed to mind. Here people are more important than clocks.

Remember when I first came and I thought I'd never be able to live here? I was so discouraged about learning the language. Now I can even understand jokes! I used to worry a lot when I met new people that I wouldn't act correctly, but now it's automatic. In fact I sometimes feel strange when I meet people from our country. I feel a little like a foreigner.

Love,

Your daughter

Letter 2

Dear John,

I can't believe I'm really living in Paris! I've already been here a week and it still seems like a dream. My friend Pierre is on vacation this week, so he's been showing me around the city. We've been to all the famous museums and churches. At night we've gone to all the bars and clubs where students hang out. Pierre helped me to find a room with a wonderful French family. They seem just like Americans. I know I'm going to feel like a member of their family in no time.

Next week classes begin. Then I'll have to start using my French more. It shouldn't be too hard.

Write soon,

Al

Letter 3

Dear Maria,

I feel like a different person than when I last wrote to you. It is as if a cloud has lifted from my head. In my last letter, things weren't going well. I didn't like people here. When I met new people, they seemed very cold and unfriendly. They didn't give me a kiss or even shake my hand. While we talked, they stood far away from me. I felt as if I had some kind of disease! Then I started watching people here and I found out that they greet everyone the way they greeted me. And when they talk to each other, they stand far away, too. One of my new friends told me that she used to think that people from my country were strange because they always wanted to stand close to her. She felt uncomfortable with them. I'm so happy to have friends here that I can really talk to about things like this. The people from our country aren't much help because they just want to sit around and complain.

You know, I'm so glad I came here. I feel like a new person. I'm much stronger than I used to be. I think that learning to live here has been the best experience of my life.

Love,

Susanna

Letter 4

My Dear Sister,

I know that you are thinking of coming here to live, but I beg you to reconsider. Life is not easy here. I thought I could come here and learn English in a few months. Then I could be a teacher again, as I was at home. But now I have been here for six months. I don't see any improvement in my English. I'm still working in our cousin's restaurant. They make it very difficult for foreigners to become teachers here.

I often think about coming home. The people here are not friendly. They don't take the time to help foreigners the way we do at home. I often feel they are laughing at me. I went to a store the other day. The owner and two of his friends were talking. They laughed when I came in the store. I walked around the store looking at things and waiting for the owner to greet me. He said nothing, so I left. I won't go there again.

I think about you and the rest of our family all the time.

With love from,

Your brother

Activity:	**Word Blitz**
Task:	To pool information about the topic of culture shock and to introduce some relevant vocabulary
Organization:	Individuals, pairs, groups
Materials:	For each student a copy of the vocabulary list on page 11
Time:	20–30 minutes
Directions:	Give the students copies of the vocabulary list and ask them to put plus (+) or minus (–) signs in front of the words according to whether they see them positively or negatively in relation to culture shock. Tell them not to worry about any vocabulary they do not understand. When they have done this, tell them to choose partners and compare their lists. Give them 10 minutes to agree on which words should be positive and which minus. Then put pairs together to make fours and ask them to repeat the process. At this point, give the meanings of any words the students are interested in.
Writing Output:	1. Pick two words on which you and your partners did not originally agree and explain your disagreement.

2. Using the following words, write a short paragraph:

change	depressed
sympathetic	friend
confident	relaxed
participate	

You may change the forms of words (nouns to verbs or adjectives, etc.)

Word Blitz Vocabulary Work Sheet

____respect
____security
____tense
____change
____insecure
____indecision
____love
____biased
____friendship
____independence
____learning
____warm
____sad
____empathy
____happy

____sympathetic
____tolerant
____thoughtful
____anger
____hostile
____overreact
____dislike
____depressed
____anxiety
____relaxed
____confident
____sensitive
____value judgment
____misperception
____peaceful

____subjective
____stereotype
____challenge
____creativity
____realistic
____unhappiness
____partnership
____identity
____frustrated
____prejudiced
____participation
____objective
____crisis
____hate
____comfortable

Activity: **Quotations**

Task: To examine several writers' reactions to cultural exposure

Organization: Individuals, pairs, groups

Materials: A large copy of each quotation on page 13, written on a separate sheet

Time: 20–30 minutes

Directions: Tape the quotations up on the wall around the classroom and ask the students to circulate and pick out the three they agree with most, and also the one they agree with least. When they have done this, ask them to find a partner who agrees with at least two of their choices and to try to reach agreement on all of their choices. Repeat this in groups of four. Then in a whole class session, compare the groups' choices.

Writing Output:

1. Choose one of the quotations and write about what it means to you.
2. Interview someone who has lived in a foreign culture and describe their experiences.

Note for Teacher: This activity is intended for students who are studying English outside their native country.

"Cultural Exposure" Quotations

1. I've learned so much about myself by living in another country.

2. I sit alone in my room and imagine I'm at home with my family. In my room there isn't any English and there isn't any snow

3. I've traveled around so much that now I don't know where I belong. I can never go home because I don't know where home is anymore.

4. I feel like I'm a citizen of the world.

5. Being a foreigner is not about looking at other people and them looking strange. It's when they look at you and you look strange.

6. There's nothing to do here. At home my friends and I went out every night. We went to a cafe and sat and talked for hours. Where can I do that here?

7. I'm tired of learning someone else's culture. I want other people to appreciate mine.

8. It's exciting to be in a foreign country, where I can be anyone I want to be.

Activity: **Situations for Discussion**

Task: To examine some situations that commonly elicit different behavior from people, depending on their cultural background.

Organization: Individuals, small groups

Materials: One copy of the situations work sheet on page 15, per student

Time: 30–40 minutes (The exercise may be adjusted to fit available time by giving fewer or more situations to discuss.)

Directions: Give each student a copy of the work sheet and ask each to complete it from their own culture's point of view. Divide them into groups of four, putting students from different cultures in each group, if possible. Give them ten minutes to compare their answers. Then ask them to try to imagine they are Americans and to respond to the same situations. Ask each group to share their answers with the class as a whole.

The students then need to compare their answers with those of native-speaker informants. This can be done in the classroom by using the teacher and/or an American guest or it can be done outside the classroom by asking each student to interview two Americans and report their answers to the class.

Writing Output:

1. Compare the reactions of Americans in one of the situations to the reactions of people from your own country

2. Write a personal account of a situation you have experienced in which either your behavior was misunderstood or you misunderstood someone else's behavior because of cultural differences.

Situations-for-Discussion Work Sheet

1. You are invited to dinner at a person's home. Just as you are leaving your house some friends of yours arrive. You should

   a) take them with you.
   b) offer them some refreshments, sit down and chat with them for a while, and then go late to dinner.
   c) explain to your friends what is happening and ask them to come back another time.
   d) call the person who invited you to dinner and explain what has happened.

2. A classmate says that you must come to his/her house for a visit some time. You

   a) leave it at that and wait for him/her to call.
   b) call him/her and set up a specific time.
   c) assume that he/she was just being polite and does not really want you to come.
   d) stop by on Sunday afternoon.

3. A friend comes to your house at holiday time and brings a wrapped present. You should

   a) say thank you and then put the present aside while you entertain your guest.
   b) make a big show of opening the present, say how much you like it, and then entertain your guest.
   c) find a present to give him/her.
   d) later in the week find a present of equivalent value to take to her.

4. You see a classmate is wearing something new that she is obviously proud of. You should

   a) show interest in the item. Ask where she bought it and how much it cost.
   b) say that you like it very much.
   c) chat to your classmate but don't mention the item.

5. You go to a restaurant with five of your classmates. Everybody has a soft drink and a hamburger. You sit and talk for a long time. Some people order more soft drinks. When it is time to leave,

   a) each person pays for her own food.
   b) you offer to pay for all of it. Your companions accept.
   c) everybody offers to pay for all of it. There is a friendly discussion about who will pay. One person finally pays for everyone.

6. You walk into a store and

   a) greet the sales clerk and other customers.
   b) greet only the clerk.
   c) wait until you are ready to purchase something before getting the attention of the clerk.

7. You are invited to dinner by a person you don't really like. You want to refuse the invitation but you don't have a good excuse for not going. You should

   a) say you'll go but don't show up.
   b) say you can't go because you have other plans.
   c) tell the person you will let him know later; then avoid him until after the dinner.
   d) tell the person you have to check your calendar and let him know. He will understand that you're not coming.

Activity:	**Finish the Sentence**
Task:	To explore the issue of culture shock
Organization:	Individuals and pairs
Materials:	One copy per person of the Finish-the-Sentence Work Sheet on page 17
Time:	20 minutes
Directions:	Give copies of the work sheet to the students and ask them to finish the sentences by themselves. As the students finish, pair them up and ask them to compare their answers. Then ask each student to pick out from their partner's responses the two they find most interesting and share them with the rest of the class.
Writing Output:	1. Write a profile of your partner. 2. Write an account of the types of responses students in your class had when they came to America. 3. Prepare a list of 10 incomplete sentences to find out your classmates' feelings about returning to their home countries.
Note to Teacher:	The work sheet refers to the United States and North Americans. If you want to use this with students who have not visited the United States any other country they have visited may be substituted.

Finish-the-Sentence Work Sheet

1. The hardest part of coming to the United States was

2. The easiest part of coming was

3. My biggest surprise was

4. My biggest disappointment was

5. The thing I dislike most about North Americans is

6. The thing I like most about North Americans is

7. The most surprising thing I have found out about myself as a result of coming to the United States is

8. My biggest mistake when dealing with North Americans was/is

9. One thing North Americans do differently is

Activity: **Stress and Sickness**

Task: To identify factors that cause stress when a person moves from one culture to another

Organization: Individuals, pairs, groups

Materials: One copy per student of the List of Stress Factors on page 19; one copy of the Answer Sheet on page 20 per each group of four students

Time: 30 minutes

Directions: Give each student a copy of the list of stress factors. Explain that these are all life events that produce stress and according to a number of studies may be causally related to certain illnesses. Ask them, working first alone and then in pairs, to put a check mark next to those they feel foreign students are likely to experience. After they have done this, ask them to rank the items they have chosen in order—from the one they think produces the most stress to the one that produces the least. Then double up the pairs of students into groups of four and ask them to produce a list that everyone in the group agrees with. Split the groups up to make different groups of four and repeat the process.

Give a copy of the answer sheet to each group and ask them to compare their order to it. Ask if people get sick more often studying overseas than in their own country. Discuss with them ways to minimize the effects of stress. Some suggestions might be: get enough sleep, exercise, and eat a well-balanced diet.

Follow-up: Ask the groups to prepare a survey to find out from foreign students how often they have been sick and the kinds of sickness they have had since arriving. They should also include questions to find the students' state of health prior to their arrival. Have them administer the survey and report to the class.

Writing Output:

1. Explain how you think foreign students could reduce their stress level.

2. Write a paragraph about the results of your survey.

List of Stress Factors

Begin or end school
Change eating habits
Have trouble with boss
Wife or mother begins or stops work
Change sleeping habits
Borrow money
Change kind of work or study
Change living conditions
Change number of arguments with spouse
Divorce
Change residence
Change social activities
Change financial status
Suffer personal illness or injury
Get married
Experience changes at place of work or study
Change responsibilities at work
Change work hours or conditions
Change schools
Change recreation habits
Change sleeping habits
Change number of family get-togethers
Separated from family

Answer Sheet: Stress Factors

Stress factors most likely to affect people traveling to another culture arranged in order of impact.

1. Separated from family
2. Experience changes at place of work
3. Change financial status
4. Change kind of work
5. Change responsibilities at work.
6. Wife or mother begins or stops work
7. Change living conditions
8. Change work hours or conditions.
9. Change residence.
10. Change school
11. Change recreation habits.
12. change number of family get-togethers
13. change eating habits

(The statistics used here are adapted from Dohrenwend, B. P. and Dohrenwend, B. S., eds., *Stressful Life Events: Their Nature and Effects*, New York, Wiley 1974.)

Activity:	**Whose Problems?**
Task:	To determine which problems experienced by foreign students are common to native students as well; to consider strategies for dealing with foreign students' problems
Organization:	Individuals, groups
Materials:	One copy per student of the work sheet on page 22
Time:	20–30 minutes
Directions:	Give students copies of the work sheet and ask them to indicate on the sheet whether they think each problem is experienced by foreign students, by native students, or by both. When they have done this individually, ask them to pair up to discuss their choices and to add to the list any other problems that they think particularly affect foreign students. In a whole-class session, ask the pairs of students to share their choices and any additions they have made to the list. Next assign each pair a problem and ask them to brainstorm what they think a person could do about it. They should then share their suggestions in a whole-class session.
Follow-Up:	Each student asks an American student to fill in the work sheet and then the class compares the American students' responses to their own.
Writing Output:	1. Choose a problem from the list that you can do something about and explain what you can do about it. 2. Compare the problems experienced by American students and foreign students entering a new class or university in the United States.

Whose Problems Work Sheet

	Foreign Student	Native Student
1. I feel very alone.		
2. I'm afraid I'm going to fail my classes.		
3. My family doesn't understand me.		
4. It's hard to make friends.		
5. I feel foolish speaking in class.		
6. The work always seems too hard.		
7. People don't behave as I expect them to.		
8. I often don't know what to say or do.		
9. Nobody seems to understand how I'm feeling		
10. It seems as if I'm two different people, one at home and one at school. I'm not sure which is the real me.		

II WORK

1. What Is Work?
2. Why Work?
3. Success Story
4. Job Shop
5. Job Match
6. Finding Your Niche
7. Job Research
8. The Perfect Applicant

Activity: **What Is Work?**

Task: To explore the characteristics of work

Organization: Individuals, pairs, groups

Materials: None

Time: 30 minutes

Directions: Dictate the following list of activities to the students:

1. Doing housework
2. Helping a friend move to a new apartment
3. Practicing the piano
4. Reading to children
5. Playing soccer
6. Cheerleading
8. Studying
9. Teaching
10. Repairing a car
11. Taking care of your own children
12. Taking care of someone else's children

Then ask the students, working individually, to put a **W** next to those that they think are work and an **N** next to those they don't think are work. Stress that you are looking for their own personal idea of what work is. After they have done this, ask them to pair up so that they can compare their lists and give reasons for their choices. Then ask each pair to define *work*. Have them complete the sentence:

Work is ___________.

Ask the students to read their definitions to the whole class and, follow up with class discussion.

Writing Output:

1. Explain what work is.

2. Explain the circumstances under which spending the day at the beach can be called work.

Activity: **Why Work?**

Task: To examine the reasons different people work

Organization: Individuals, groups, whole class

Materials: A copy for each student of the handout on page 27 (or write the list on the board)

Time: 25–35 minutes

Directions: Give the students a copy of the Why-Do-People-Work list. Ask them to pick out the six that are most important to them and to rank them in order of importance from #1 (the most important) to #6 (the least important). While the students are doing this, put the list on the board or overhead projector and add *1st, 2nd, 3rd* and *total* as shown below.

	1st	2nd	3rd	Total
To make money				
To meet interesting people				
To use their minds or bodies				
To feel important				
To develop themselves				
To help society				
To have power				
To get out of the house				
To have something to do				
To avoid being bored				
To enjoy free time more				
To get a good pension				

When the students have finished, fill in the chart with the numbers of students who made each choice, starting with how many students made item A their first choice and going on to how many made it their second choice, etc. Use the chart to focus discussion on areas of difference.

Writing Output:

1. Use the chart to help you write an account of why people work.

2. Interview five people outside of class about why they work, and write a summary of your findings.

Why Do People Work?

A. To make money

B. To meet interesting people

C. To use their minds and/or bodies

D. To feel important

E. To develop themselves

F. To help society

G. To have power

H. To get out of the house

I. To have something to do everyday

J. To avoid being bored

K. To enjoy free time more

L. To get a good pension at retirement

Activity:	**Success Story**
Task:	To discuss the work ethic
Organization:	Pairs, groups
Materials:	A copy of the story on page 29 for each student
Time:	15–20 minutes
Directions:	Give the story to the students and ask them to read it. Then divide the class into groups of four and ask half the groups to discuss the story from the man's point of view and half from the boy's point of view. When they have done this put them in pairs in which one student represents the man's point of view and the other the boy's point of view. Ask them to discuss the story.
Writing Output:	1. Tell the story from your partner's point of view. 2. Who do you think was right, the beach boy or the businessman? Explain why.

Anecdote

A successful businessman was walking along the beach in Naples when he saw a local boy very poorly dressed lying on the beach. The man immediately urged him to get up and make something of himself. "Go find a job," he said, "and save as much money as you can. Pretty soon you'll be able to buy a small boat and earn more money selling fish. And, if you continue to save, in time you'll be able to buy a bigger boat and catch more fish so that you can buy an even bigger boat and then a second boat and a third boat, until finally you'll own a whole fleet of boats and be rich.

" And then I'll be able to lie on the beach in Naples," said the boy.

Activity: **Job Shop**

Task: To examine the types of jobs that are available and to give students an opportunity to consider which types of jobs they are attracted to

Organization: Individuals, pairs, groups

Materials: A copy of the job list on page 31 for each student, plus a blank sheet of paper.

Time: 30 minutes

Directions: Give each student a copy of the job list and ask the students to group together on a separate piece of paper the jobs they feel are related. Then ask them, first in pairs and then in fours, to compare and revise their groupings and to give a heading to each group. Finally ask them to consider the group to which they personally would like to belong.

Writing Output:

1. Describe the group of jobs you are most attracted to and explain why.

2. Choose one group of jobs and explain how they are related to each other.

Job List

Truck driver	Cashier	Musician
Sales clerk	Auto mechanic	Film director
Aerobics instructor	Zoo keeper	Clown
Physiotherapist	Secretary	Translator
Telephone operator	Singer	Veterinarian
Religious leader	Child care worker	Housewife/husband
Actor	Architect	Designer
Pharmacist	Inventor	Plumber
Computer programmer	Factory worker	Gardener
Electrician	Medical researcher	Artist
Botanist	Carpenter	Physicist
Garbage collector	Accountant	Athlete
Politician	Doctor	Journalist
Dentist	Soldier	Lawyer
Engineer	Pilot	Psychiatrist
Construction worker	Novelist	Insurance salesman
Nurse	Police officer	Firefighter
Teacher	Social worker	Realtor
Bricklayer	Photographer	Counselor
Librarian	Banker	Telephone engineer

Activity: **Job Match**

Task: To examine the characteristics of different jobs

Organization: Individuals, groups

Materials: One copy of the job list on page 31 and one copy of the adjective list on page 33 for each student.

Time: 30 minutes

Directions: Give the students the list of jobs and the list of adjectives. Tell them to match the adjectives to the jobs using each adjective at least once and ascribing at least one adjective to each job. When a few students have finished and before interest dies, put the students into groups and get them to compare their answers.

Writing Output:

1. Choose one job and describe the kind of person that would be good at it.

2. Choose another job and tell what you think a person with that job does all day.

Adjectives List

mechanical	routine	athletic	autonomous
responsible	professional	skillful	helpful
educated	well-trained	quick	slow
repetitive	creative	white-collar	underpaid
blue-collar	well-paid	prestigious	glamorous
career	indoor	outdoor	analytical
caring	clerical	mathematical	detailed
precise	exciting	social	persuasive
influential	entertaining	inspiring	artistic
people-oriented	productive	investigative	innovative
problem-solving	informative	enlightening	boring
manufacturing	supervisory	fun	

Activity: **Finding Your Niche**

Task: To consider personal characteristics in relation to jobs

Organization: Individuals, pairs

Materials: A copy of the work sheet on page 35 for every student and one copy of the job list from Job Shop on page 31, for each pair of students

Time: 30 minutes

Directions: Give the students the work sheets and ask them to fill them in individually. Explain that each of the items shows two opposite points of view with a graded line between them. Students should circle the line at the point at which it roughly approximates their point of view. Take for example, the imaginary item below

I love ice cream 1 2 3 4 5 6 7 I hate ice cream

If I love ice cream, I will circle the line at point 1; and if I hate it, I will circle the line at point 7. If I am neutral, I will circle the line at point 4; but if I like it just a little I will circle point 3, etc. As the students finish, put them into pairs and ask them to study each other's answer sheets. On the basis of the information on the sheet, each student should then suggest three jobs for the other person. Copies of the job list may be provided as an aid.

Writing Output:

1. Explain and give reasons based on your partner's answer sheet why one of the jobs you chose was suitable for your partner.
2. Choose a job from the job list and, using the answer sheet, explain which characteristics fit the job.

Finding-Your-Niche Work Sheet

1. I like to work alone.	1 2 3 4 5 6 7	I like to work with people.
2. I like to have a lot of responsibility.	1 2 3 4 5 6 7	I don't like to have a lot of responsibility.
3. Status is important to me.	1 2 3 4 5 6 7	Status is not important to me.
4. I like to be creative.	1 2 3 4 5 6 7	I am not concerned with being creative.
5. I like to work without supervision.	1 2 3 4 5 6 7	I like someone to tell me what to do.
6. I like to supervise others.	1 2 3 4 5 6 7	I don't like telling others what to do.
7. I like to work under pressure	1 2 3 4 5 6 7	I don't like to work under pressure.
8. I like a routine job.	1 2 3 4 5 6 7	I like a job where there is always something new.
9. I like to put most of my energy into my job.	1 2 3 4 5 6 7	I like to put most of my time into my social life.
10. I like to stay in one place all day.	1 2 3 4 5 6 7	I don't like to stay in one place all day.
11. I like a clearly defined job.	1 2 3 4 5 6 7	I don't like a clearly defined job.
12. I like to help others.	1 2 3 4 5 6 7	I would not like a job that involves helping others.
13. I like making decisions.	1 2 3 4 5 6 7	I don't like making decisions.
14. I like a job with a future.	1 2 3 4 5 6 7	I'm not concerned about the future.
15. I take pride in my work.	1 2 3 4 5 6 7	It is not important to me to be able to take pride in my work.
16. I like to see immediate results in my work.	1 2 3 4 5 6 7	I don't care if I see immediate results.

Activity: **Job Research**

Purpose: To seek out and share information about specific jobs

Organization: Pairs, groups, whole class

Materials: None

Time: Two class periods plus homework

Directions: Divide the class into groups of four and ask each group to choose a job they are particularly interested in. Then tell them that they are going to be asked to write an information leaflet about that job. Ask them to draw up a list of at least 10 interview questions that they could ask someone in that job. Ask them to share their questions in a whole class session. Next, ask the whole class to brainstorm other possible sources of information about the jobs (e.g., library, school counselor, career center, etc.). Ask each group to seek out information from one of the sources about the job.

In a later session, ask the members of the group to share the information they have collected and to write the leaflet as a collaborative effort. The leaflets should each contain a description of the job, plus information about how students can best prepare themselves for this job.The leaflets are then passed around and read by the other groups.

Writing Output:

1. Write a letter applying for one of the jobs your class gathered information about. Explain why you would be good for the job.

2. Which of the jobs interests you least? Explain why.

Activity: **The Perfect Applicant**

Task: To explore the characteristics that determine whether or not an applicant gets a particular job

Organization: Groups, whole class

Materials: Copy of an employment want ad per group

Time: 30–40 minutes

Directions: Divide the class into groups of four and give each group a copy of the want ad. Choose one group to be the employers. Explain that in 15 minutes they will interview the candidates for the job. In the meantime, they have to decide the kind of person they are looking for and the interview questions they will need to ask. The other groups each represent an applicant for the job. Each group should try to invent the perfect applicant, bearing in mind age, sex, marital status, family, educational background, and experience. They should invent a list of jobs and related experience that their candidate has had in the past that make him or her particularly suitable for this job. When each group has invented its candidate's personal and job history, ask them to chose one group member to be the candidate in the job interviews.

With the whole class watching, ask the employers to take turns interviewing the candidates. When all the candidates have been interviewed, the employers have five minutes to choose the person they will hire while the other groups decide who they think will get the job. Then the employers report back on who is the successful candidate and, if necessary, defend their choice. (If a video camera is available the interviews can be recorded and played back later.) Class discussion centers around whether the right applicant got the job.

Writing Output:

1. Describe the applicant your group invented for the job. What made him/her a good choice?

2. Explain the pros and cons of interviews as a way to choose someone for a job.

III LANGUAGE LEARNING

1. Wall Quotes
2. Finish the Sentence
3. Self-Assessment
4. Vocabulary Memorization
5. Rate the Activities
6. The Language of the Classroom
7. Dying Words
8. Successful Language Learners
9. Letter Response

Activity: **Wall Quotes**

Task: To pick out quotes students identify with

Organization: Individuals, pairs

Materials: Copies of quotes (see below) large enough to post on the wall with room for students to sign up

Time: 20 minutes

Directions: Post the following quotes around the room before the students come in:

- I always have trouble speaking English with a person who speaks my native language fluently.
- I can't be good friends with a person who doesn't share my native language.
- When I speak English I am not really me. I don't know enough English yet to be me.
- Jokes in English aren't funny.
- It is harder to talk on the telephone than face to face.

Ask them to walk around the room and sign the quotation they identify with most. Then ask them to find a partner and explain their choice to their partner.

Writing Output:

1. Pick the quotation that you identify with most and explain why it is that you identify with it.

2. You cannot learn a language without learning some of the culture. Agree or disagree.

Activity: **Finish the Sentence**

Task: To explore students' perceptions of themselves when they speak English

Organization: Individuals, whole class, groups

Materials: None

Time: 30 minutes

Directions: Ask each student to write a sentence on the board beginning,

"When I speak English, I ______________________________."

After all the sentences are on the board, working with the whole class, ask the students to:

1. Check the sentences for mistakes and to suggest corrections.

2. Erase any sentences that are not relevant.

3. Choose between sentences that are saying the same thing and eliminate one from the board.

Then ask the students to break up into groups of four to complete the following tasks:

4. Group together sentences that are related.

5. Make a topic sentence for each group of sentences.

Writing Output:

1. By adding additional sentences and linking words, write a paragraph entitled "Speaking English."

2. Do you act differently when you speak English? If so, describe how you change.

Activity: **Self-Assessment**

Task: To chart progress in ESL and provide the teacher with feedback about needs and aspirations; to give the students more sense of control over their language learning

Organization: Individuals, pairs

Materials: None

Time: 15 minutes

Directions: Ask the students to make a list of 10 things they can do in English. Then ask them to make a list of 10 things that they can't do now but would like to be able to do (They may set a time period here for when they would like to be able to do these things.) Get them to pair up to talk about things they could do to speed up reaching their goals.

Follow-Up: This is a useful activity to repeat periodically so that students can see their progress and make new goals.

Writing Output:

1. Write about your greatest achievements so far in learning English.

2. Choose one of your language learning goals and write a plan for achieving it.

Activity:	**Vocabulary Memorization**
Task:	To try out techniques for memorizing vocabulary
Organization:	Individuals, groups, whole class
Materials:	A copy of the vocabulary list on page 45 on the overhead projector
Time:	30–40 minutes

Directions:

Give the students two minutes to memorize as many items as they can from the list on the overhead projector. Then have them write down all the items they can remember. After checking their results, put the students in groups of four so that each group contains at least one of the students who performed best on the memory test. Tell them that you are going to give them another chance to memorize the words. This time, however, the members of the groups will not get individual scores but will each get the average score of all the members of the group. This means that the better the other members of the group do on the test, the better each person's score will be.

Tell the students that they will have 10 minutes to memorize the words and that they can coach one another, share techniques, etc. Make sure that they realize that this is a group task, not an individual one. Offer a reward for the *group* that performs best. When the time is up, retest the students to see which group performs best. Ask them to share any techniques that worked. If the following suggestions do not occur, suggest them yourself: putting the words in sentences together, relating the word to a similar word in your own language, grouping them together, imaging, mnemonic devices. Give the students one last chance, using any technique they like, to try to memorize the words. Reward everyone!

Writing Output:

1. Describe the technique you think works best.
2. Write about EFL/ESL classes in your school using at least five items from the vocabulary list.

Language-Learning Vocabulary List

foreign language	pronunciation	oral
group	pair	word
mother tongue	listen	speak
read	write	error
teacher	language	learner
learning style	motivation	mistake
content	practice	active
meaning	meaningless	passive
communicate	objective	syllabus
strategy	task	sentence
interact	understand	syllable
native language	paragraph	individual
native speaker		

Activity: **Rate the Activities**

Task: To compare the value of various kinds of classroom activities from the point of view of the student and of the teacher

Organization: Whole class, individuals, groups

Materials: A copy of the questionnaire on page 47 for each student plus a copy of the graph for each group of four students

Time:

First lesson 30 minutes
Second lesson 30 minutes
Plus homework interview

Directions: Brainstorm with the students the different types of learning activities that go on in the classroom. Then give each student a copy of the prepared Activities list on page 47 and ask them to rank the items in order of importance. Ask them to form groups to compare their choices and record the average score the group gave each item. After they have done this, give each group a copy of the graph on page 47, allowing them 10 minutes to work out what the graph shows and to pick out any information they find surprising.

In a whole-class session, let the groups compare what they have found. The ensuing discussion should focus on differences in how teachers and students value the activities. Ask the students whether they think their own teachers would rank the activities in the same way. For homework, ask students to have other ESL/Language teachers rank the activities and explain why they rank them as they do. In the next class the students, working in the same groups as the day before, make a graph of their group's average scores and the average scores of the teachers they interviewed.

Writing Output:

1. Use your graph to help you describe your results.
2. Choose one of the items that teachers and students valued differently and explain the teacher's point of view.

(This idea was originally described as an action research project in Nunan, D., *The Learner-Centered Curriculum: A Study in Second Language Teaching*, Cambridge University Press, Cambridge, United Kingdom 1976.)

Teaching Activities

Please rank the following teaching activities from 1 to 12 according to how useful you think they are in learning a language:

____Group and pair work

____Translation

____Grammatical explanation in *native* language

____Grammatical explanation in *target* language

____Teacher correction of errors

____Games and songs

____Homework

____Listening to tapes

____Drills

____Memorizing sentences/ dialogues, etc.

____Writing compositions

____Reading

Sample Student/Teacher Evaluation of Activities

[International School of Curacao 1988]

——— Students' Evaluation of Activities

▬▬▬ Teachers' Evaluation of Activities

5 = very valuable   1 = not valuable at all

	1	2	3	4	5
Group and Pair Work					
Translation					
Grammatical Explanation in the Native Language					
Grammatical Explanation in the Target Language					
Teacher Correction of Errors					
Games and Songs					
Homework					
Listening to tapes					
Drills					
Memorizing Sentences/Dialogues, etc.					
Writing Compositions					
Reading					

Activity: **The Language of the Classroom**

Task: To explore the use of the students' native language in the classroom

Organization: Small groups

Materials: None

Time: 20–30 minutes

Directions: Write on the board: "English will be spoken at all times."

Tell the students that they are to consider this a new class rule. Then divide the class up into groups of four. Explain that half of the groups will consider the rule from the point of view of a teacher, while the other half will consider it from the point of view of a student. Designate which groups will take which viewpoint. Each group should be ready to explain the rule from their person's viewpoint. When they have done this, regroup them so that each point of view is equally represented in each group. Ask them to explain their differing points of view to each other.

Writing Output:

1. Write about using the students' native language in the classroom: first from the point of view of the teacher, and second from the point of view of the students.

2. You have recently come to America from Tanzania and your child is in an ESL class in the local school. Your child tells you that he does not understand what is happening in the classroom because many of the other students are using their native language instead of English. Write a letter to the school principal complaining about the situation.

Activity: **Dying Words**

Task: To brainstorm the language necessary for survival in a foreign culture

Organization: Pairs, groups, whole class

Materials: None

Time: 15–20 minutes

Directions: Present the following situation to the class:

> You have just arrived in an alien culture. The only interpreter you have is dying. He has only five minutes to live. What would you ask him?

Give the students five minutes in pairs to produce a list of items they would need translations for. When they have done this, double up the pairs into groups of four and give them 10 minutes to produce together a final list that they all agree on. In whole-class discussion, get the groups to report back their choices. Ask them also to suggest any other factors that might influence their choices (e.g., Are the natives friendly? Are they in the town or the country?).

Writing Output:

1. Explain why you chose the items you did.
2. What language items would a person coming to your country need to know? Explain why.

Activity: **Successful Language Learners**

Task:

1. To divide a list of language learning strategies into two groups: those that the students think will lead to success and those that will not
2. To read about successful language learning
3. To match student comments to points in the reading passage

Organization: Individuals, small groups

Materials: Individual copies of the work sheets on page 52. The student profiles can be printed or recorded for listening comprehension practice

Time:

First lesson	30 minutes
Second lesson	30 minutes

Directions: This is a three-part exercise. Before meeting in small groups, the students should read the list of strategies. In small groups and with as little teacher intervention as possible, students should clarify any parts of the list that they do not understand. Then the group should divide the list into two parts: those strategies that they believe lead to success in language learning and those that do not. The process of coming to agreement on the list will help them gain insights into their own strategies for language learning. Next, the students should read the passage on language learning individually. They should then return to their groups to discuss their earlier decisions in light of what they have read. Finally, they should read or listen to the student profiles and decide which students are likely to be successful and why.

Writing Output:

1. Choose the strategy you find most helpful and explain how you put it to use.
2. What makes some of your classmates learn English faster than others?

Quiz on Language Learning Strategies

Divide the following items into two groups: those that you think would help you to learn a language and those that you think would not be helpful.

1. Spend most of your time with friends from your own country.
2. Try to think in English.
3. Look up every word you don't know in the dictionary.
4. Ask your friends to translate for you in class so that you don't miss anything.
5. Spend as much time as possible practicing the language.
6. Don't worry about people laughing at you when you speak the language.
7. Blame your teacher if you don't learn as quickly and well as you would like.
8. Don't be discouraged when people don't understand you.
9. Spend all your time studying.
10. Listen carefully in class but don't talk.
11. Speak English to your classmates outside of class.
12. Use movies, trips to the supermarket, telephone calls, traffic tickets, etc., as opportunities for learning English.

Reading: Successful Language Learning

Although we cannot predict exactly who will be successful in learning a language, successful language learners seem to have a number of characteristics in common.

1. Most successful language learners have a good idea of how they learn best. They are able to adapt different methods and styles of teaching to suit their own best way of learning. This permits them to get the most out of any learning situation, whether it is a class, a laboratory, homework, or a party at which everyone speaks English.

2. Successful learners usually like the language and the people who speak it. They try to imagine what it is like to be a native speaker. This helps them feel less self-conscious when they copy the pronunciation and gestures of native speakers. It also helps them to think in the language. Some experts even suggest that the best way to learn a language is to fall in love with a native speaker of that language. This is not, of course, necessary.

3. Good language learners try to use the language as much as possible and in as many ways as possible. Most experts agree that we learn what we practice. Therefore, students who speak the language often, even with a lot of mistakes, will eventually speak it well. This also applies to other language skills. Students who read a lot will learn to read well, but they may still have trouble speaking. Students who spend all their time looking up words in the dictionary will become good at looking up words, but may not be able to speak or understand the language easily.

4. Most successful language learners are good at guessing the meanings of unknown words. We all do this without thinking about it in our own language, but many learners do not want to try guessing in a foreign language. They prefer to find exact meanings in a dictionary. These people remain very slow readers and have difficulty in listening comprehension.

5. Most successful language learners understand that when they are learning a language, they are going to make mistakes. They do not wait to be able to say something perfectly, but try to use the language that they know in order to express themselves. If other people do not understand them, they try again in a different way.

Student Profiles

Bob: I don't like my French class. It's boring. We do the same thing every day. My teacher is always mad at me because I never do my homework. It's a waste of time.

Eddie: I don't like to practice Spanish with my classmates. They're all Americans like me. Why should I talk to them in Spanish?

Lorrie: I have a lot of friends here who speak Spanish. When I hear people talking Spanish at the cafeteria or the recreation center or anywhere, I go up to them and introduce myself. Some of my friends say I'm crazy, but I'm learning more Spanish than they are.

Susan: At first I was afraid that people would think I was stupid when I spoke to them in French. After all, I was using very simple words — just like a little kid. But I decided I had to do it. Now I feel better about it. I can talk about a lot of things and people usually understand me.

George: I never speak Spanish except when I'm in class. I'm afraid that Spanish speakers will laugh at me when I make mistakes — or maybe they won't understand me and I'll have to repeat everything.

Activity: **Letter Response**

Task: To explore solutions for language learning problems

Organization: Whole class, pairs, groups

Materials: One copy of the letter per person

Time: 20–30 minutes

Directions: Talk with the students about how they felt when they first went to a foreign country. Could they speak the language? Did anyone give them any good advice? Etc. Then give a copy of the letter to each student and ask them to read it. After they have done this, they should pair up and answer the letter. Then ask them to form groups of four and compare their letters.

Writing Output:

1. Write another letter from Mike three months after the first one.

2. Share the best piece of advice that you were ever given about learning other languages.

Answering a Letter

Paris,
France

Dear ________________,

I really don't know what to do. I've been in Paris for two weeks now and I don't understand a word anyone says to me. The only time I get to talk is when I speak English with friends from the States. I really want to learn French but I don't know how to begin. I know you learned English very well and quickly, so I'm hoping you'll give me some advice. Please write as soon as possible.

Best wishes,

Mike

IV RELATIONSHIPS

1. What's Important in a Friend?
2. Dear Sarah
3. Drawing a Sociogram
4. Cinderella Vocabulary
5. Family Proverbs
6. The Trust Game
7. Marriage Roles Questionnaire
8. Group Dynamics

Activity: **What's Important in a Friend?**

Task: To explore what qualities are valuable in a friend

Organization: Individuals, pairs, whole class

Materials: A copy of the handout on page 60 for every student

Time: 20 minutes

Directions: Give each student a copy of the list and ask them to give the number 1 to the quality they find most important in friendship and the number 12 to the one they find least important and to rank the other qualities in between. Ask them also to add any items they think are missing from the list. Then, first in pairs and then in small groups, have them compare their choices. (If possible, the groups should include both sexes.) In a whole-class discussion, have the students report back on any other qualities they would like to add to the list and any disagreements they found within their groups.

Follow-Up:

1. Interview a person from another culture to see how that person ranks the qualities on the list.

2. Interview two boys and two girls from the same ethnic background. Do they give equal value to the qualities or are there any gender-related differences?

Writing Output:

1. Describe your best friend in terms of the qualities on the list.

2. Compare the qualities males and females value in a friend.

What's Important in a Friend?

A good friend:

is a good listener.

keeps my secrets.

is loyal.

is affectionate.

agrees with me.

helps me when I have problems.

always tells me the truth.

accepts me as I am.

has a sense of humor.

always has time for me.

likes to do the same things I do.

Activity: **Dear Sarah**

Task: To examine a breakdown in a relationship from both points of view

Organization: Pairs

Materials: A copy of both of the following letters for each pair of students

Time: 30 minutes

Directions: Give Letter A to half the class and Letter B to the other half. Allow the students 10 minutes to read their letter and to discuss it with a partner who has the same letter. Then take away the letters and put the students in new pairs, in which the students have read different letters. Ask the students to take turns in explaining the situation to each other from their letter's point of view. Then ask them to think of any possible solutions that would please both writers.

Writing Output:

1. Choose one of the letters and reply to it.
2. Write about how you lost a friend.

Dear Sarah

Letter A

Dear Sarah,

Sue and I have been best friends since we were in 1st Grade. We did everything together and always had a great time. Just recently she's started spending a lot of time with other people and she seems almost as friendly with them as she is with me. She's acting as if our relationship isn't special but just like all her other relationships. What should I do?

Letter B

Dear Sarah,

What can I do about a clingy friend? I really like her and we've been friends for years but she wants the two of us to do everything together, just like when we were 6 years old. I need other friends as well, but I don't want to hurt her feelings.

Activity: **Drawing a Sociogram**

Task: To think about different relationships.

Organization: Individuals, pairs

Materials: None

Time: 20 minutes

Directions: Ask the students to brainstorm in pairs a list of people they have relationships with (e.g., teacher, sister, neighbor, classmate, partner). After they have done this, ask them working individually to draw a dot in the center of the paper to represent themselves. The next step is to arrange symbols representing other people around the dot according to their relationship with them. The closer the friend, the closer they should be represented on the picture to the central dot. When they have completed this task individually, ask them to explain their diagram to their partner.

Writing Output:

1. Write about what your partner told you.
2. Write about a relationship in which the person has become closer or more distant. Explain what caused this.

Activity: **Cinderella Vocabulary**

Task: To think about words that are used to describe character

Organization: Individual, pairs

Materials: Copies of the vocabulary list on page 65

Time: 30 minutes

Directions: Ask the students if they have ever heard the story of Cinderella. If they have, tell them to listen to see if your story is exactly the same as the story they know. Tell the class the story of Cinderella. Ask them afterwards to tell you any differences. Then give each student a copy of the vocabulary list and ask them, working in pairs, to make a list of the characters and to decide which vocabulary words go with each character. They may use words more than once and they may also leave out any they do not consider suitable. When they have finished, ask each of them to think of a story from their culture about relationships and tell it to their partners.

Writing Output:

1. Write down the story that your partner told you.
2. Describe your best friend, using items of vocabulary from the list.

Cinderella Vocabulary List

cooperative	helpful	competitive
friendly	destructive	trusting
playful	funny	likable
angry	loving	aggressive
sympathetic	respectful	supportive
superior	confident	creative
dependent	ignorant	independent
inferior	practical	open-minded
prejudiced	self-centered	optimistic
honest	generous	relaxed
intelligent	idealistic	tolerant

Activity: **Family Proverbs**

Task: To examine attitudes toward relatives

Organization: Individuals, pairs, groups

Materials: Proverbs list on page 67 written on large sheets of paper and put up on the walls

Time: 20 minutes

Directions: Ask the students to circulate and sign their names on the proverbs that they like best, then to find a partner and explain to them why they chose the ones they did.

Writing Output:

1. Take a proverb from your own language and translate it into English. Then explain what it means.
2. Choose a proverb from the list and write a story that illustrates it.

Family Proverbs

1. Relatives are scorpions.
2. My brother and I against my cousin, my cousin and I against a stranger.
3. Your relative may eat your flesh, but they will not break your bones.
4. No one can make you suffer like a brother.
5. Relatives love each other as long as they are rich.
6. Relatives and cats are all ungrateful.
7. Relatives and the sun: the farther away the better.
8. The mother-in-law doesn't remember that she was once a daughter-in-law.
9. Home is where when you have to go there they have to take you in.

Activity: **The Trust Game**

Task: To explore the issue of trust in relationships

Organization: Pairs, whole class

Materials: A large version of the chart below

Time: 10–15 minutes

Directions: Ask the students if they have ever played the game "Scissors, paper, stone." If anyone has, ask them to explain to the others how it is played. Then explain that they are going to be playing a related game in class today: They will play the game in pairs and each person has two choices—to bring their hand out from from behind their back either open or as a fist. Put the chart up on the wall and explain the scoring. If both students bring out open hands then both students receive 2 points. If one student brings out an open palm and the other student brings out a fist then the student with the open palm will receive 0 points and the student with the fist will receive 4 points. If both students bring out fists, then both will receive 1 point.

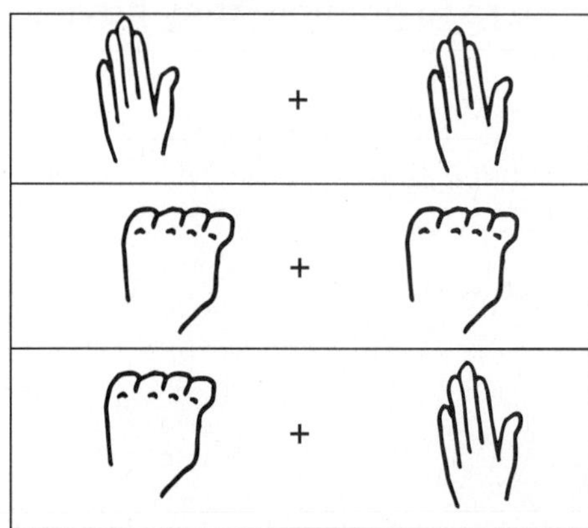

= 2 points each

= 1 point each

= 4 points for the fist
0 points for the open palm

Have one pair of students demonstrate the game and then ask the students to play the game for five minutes in pairs. After they have done this, ask them to report back. Make sure that the whole-class discussion brings out the following points: Was it enjoyable? What usually happened? Why? What would be the best way to play the game for both players? What has the way the game was played to do with trust?

Writing Output:

1. Explain what happened when you played the game.
2. Think about a person you trust. What is it about that person that makes you trust them?

(This game was described in Richardson, R., *Learning for Change in World Society*, World Studies Project, London, United Kingdom, 1976.)

Activity: **Marriage Roles Questionnaire**

Task: To explore the roles of husband and wife

Organization: Individuals, pairs, groups

Materials: A copy of the questionnaire for each student

Time: 15–20 minutes

Directions: Give each student a copy of the questionnaire on page 70 and ask them to complete it. After they have done this, ask them to compare their answers first in pairs and then in groups of four.

Writing Output:

1. Choose a question that there was disagreement on within your group. Write a paragraph explaining the issue from your point of view. Then write a paragraph explaining the issue from the other person's point of view

2. Compare a husband's role in the United States to a husband's role in your culture.

(This questionnaire grew out of one prepared by Elaine Aydin at the Turco British Association, Ankara, Turkey.)

Behavior Within Marriage

1. Who should do which tasks?
   (a) All jobs in the home are suitable for both husband and wife.
   (b) Men can do things such as food shopping, but housework and child care aren't suitable for them.
   (c) Jobs such as washing, cooking, and cleaning are the wife's responsibility.

2. If a wife has a full-time job, how should the housework be divided?
   (a) Her husband should do half the housework.
   (b) He should help with some jobs.
   (c) He shouldn't be expected to help with housework if he doesn't want to.

3. If you saw a woman washing the family car, what would you think?
   (a) It's not a suitable job for a woman.
   (b) Why isn't the husband doing it?
   (c) What a helpful wife!

4. Who should get up first and make breakfast?
   (a) The wife—it's part of her duty.
   (b) The husband, because the wife makes the other meals.
   (c) They should do it together.

5. Should married couples ever spend evenings apart?
   (a) Yes, why not?
   (b) It's all right if they are visiting their families.
   (c) It's all right for the husband but not for the wife.

6. Does a husband have a right to tell his wife what to wear?
   (a) Yes.
   (b) Only if she can tell him what to wear.

7. Should a woman keep her own salary for things such as clothes, makeup, and hairdresser.
   (a) No, her salary should be part of the family income.
   (b) It's a good idea if the family can afford it.
   (c) Yes.

8. How should a woman vote?
   (a) A woman doesn't know anything about politics so she should vote as her husband does.
   (b) If a woman disagrees with her husband over politics, then she shouldn't vote.
   (c) A woman should vote for whatever party she likes.

Activity: **Group Dynamics**

Task: To examine the roles played within a group

Organization: Groups of six

Materials: Each group will need: a die, a pair of scissors, a set of crayons, a large sheet of white paper, two smaller sheets of colored paper, and a role card (see page 72) for each group member.

Time: 30–40 minutes

Directions: Divide the class into groups of six and give each group a set of materials, excluding the role cards. Then explain that they have 15 minutes to devise a game using these materials. They are to write down the rules of the game, so that the other members of the class will be able to play it. Tell them that each person will also receive some additional written instructions to follow that they must not show to anyone else. Give out one role card per student and then give them time to complete the assigned task.

When they have completed the task, explain that you gave everybody a role card telling them the type of person they had to be and the type of behavior they had to use. Ask them to stay in their groups and guess what was on each others' cards.

Writing Output:

1. Write a paragraph explaining the role you usually play in group discussion.

2. Choose one group member that you found especially hard to deal with. What was it that made working together difficult?

Role Cards

Role Card 1

You are a person who hates to argue about anything. You try to avoid conflict by agreeing with everyone.

Role Card 2

You are a person who gets angry with people who disagree with you.

Role Card 3

You are a person who likes to make jokes about everything.

Role Card 4

You are someone who enjoys arguments.

Role Card 5

Be yourself.

Role Card 6

Be yourself.

V EDUCATION

1. Draw the School
2. Picture It in Words
3. What Makes a Good Student?
4. Classroom Behavior
5. Discipline Blues
6. Academic Problems Questionnaire
7. Agree/Disagree Snowball
8. Edco

Activity:	**Draw the School**
Task:	To explore students' perceptions of their own school.
Organization:	Individuals, pairs
Materials:	One sheet of blank paper for each student (the bigger the better)
Time:	30 minutes
Directions:	Give each student a sheet of paper and a pencil and ask them to draw a picture of the school as they see it. Make it clear that good drawing is not necessary and that what you're interested in is their perspective. As the students finish, pair them up and ask them to discuss their pictures with their partner.
Alternative:	The students could draw the pictures together in pairs and discuss as they draw.
Follow-Up:	It's a good idea to hold onto the student pictures for "Picture It in Words," the next activity.
Writing Output:	1. Describe your favorite place in the school. 2. Compare the way you see your school with the way your partner sees it.

Activity: **Picture It in Words**

Task: To explore vocabulary associated with school

Organization: Individuals, pairs, groups

Materials: A copy of the Education Vocabulary Sheet on page 77 for every student. A picture of the school for every student, plus enough extra pictures for three quarters of the class to have a second copy. (This should be a simple line drawing either taken from one of the student's pictures produced in "Draw the School" or drawn by the teacher and duplicated.)

Time: 20–30 minutes

Directions: Give each student a copy of the vocabulary list and the picture of the school. Ask the students to read through the vocabulary list and to pick out and write at least 20 words on the picture wherever they feel is most appropriate. Then ask them in pairs to repeat the process using a blank picture in such a way that they both agree with the selection and placement of the words. Then double up the pairs into groups of four and ask them to repeat the process one more time, again reaching consensus on the selection and the placement of the words.

Alternative: Instead of using printed vocabulary sheet, the teacher can select a more limited list.

Writing Output:

1. Is there any location where you put more than one word? If so, explain why these words belong together in that place.

2. Choose a place in your school and write a paragraph about what goes on there and how you feel there.

Education Vocabulary List

elementary	teacher	peer pressure
practical	students	choice
positive	classroom	participation
beliefs	college	student-centered
curriculum	career	multicultural
freedom	creative	teacher-centered
ideas	intelligence	self-esteem
knowledge	understanding	change
caring	school	homework
society	world	developing
academic	grades	pass
fail	succeed	roles
sex	kindness	employment
vocational	community	mixing
goals	needs	boring
study	thinking	organize
discuss	sharing	growth
dropout	training	socialization
active	passive	inspiration
repeat	learning	secondary
textbook	tests	university
graduate	vacation	

Activity:	**What Makes a Good Student?**
Task:	To compare the viewpoints that teachers and students have about the characteristics of a good student
Organization:	Pairs and groups
Materials:	Two copies per student of the survey sheet on page 7
Time:	Lesson 1: 20–30 minutes Lesson 2: 20–30 minutes

Directions:

Give each student a copy of the survey and ask them to fill it in. Next, ask them to compare their answers in groups and to use their individual scores to work out a group average for each characteristic. Then use these scores to work out a class average for each characteristic. Discuss whether they think a group of teachers would make the same choices. Finally, distribute the extra copies of the survey and ask them to survey a teacher before the next class. (Surveying may be done individually or in pairs, depending on the availability of teachers and the level of confidence of the students).

In the next class, work out the average teacher score for each characteristic. Ask the students, in groups, to compare the teachers' scores and the students' scores and to discuss any differences. (An effective way to do this would be to graph the two sets of scores.)

Writing Output:

1. Report the results of the survey.
2. Find instances of students and teachers disagreeing, and try to explain why they disagree.

Good Student Survey

Rate the following characteristics according to how important they are to being a good student.

1 = not at all important
2 = very important
3 = neutral

Is good at sports	1	2	3	4	5
Participates in class	1	2	3	4	5
Is neat	1	2	3	4	5
Does well in tests	1	2	3	4	5
Is motivated	1	2	3	4	5
Is intelligent	1	2	3	4	5
Works hard	1	2	3	4	5
Asks questions	1	2	3	4	5
Does good written work	1	2	3	4	5
Is active in class	1	2	3	4	5
Listens to what the teacher says and is able to repeat it back in tests	1	2	3	4	5
Does not disagree with the teacher	1	2	3	4	5
Gets along well with other students	1	2	3	4	5
Is quiet in class	1	2	3	4	5
Always does what the teacher says	1	2	3	4	5
Speaks a lot in class	1	2	3	4	5
Can argue his/her point of view	1	2	3	4	5

Activity: **Classroom Behavior**

Task: To explore the issue of appropriate behavior in the classroom

Organization: Individuals, groups

Materials: A copy of the chart on page 81 for each student

Time: 15–20 minutes

Directions: Give each student a copy of the chart and ask them to fill it out individually. After they have done this, ask them to compare their responses in groups.

Writing Output:

1. Think of examples of inappropriate classroom behavior. Explain why you consider them inappropriate. Then give your paper to a classmate from a different country and ask her to write you a reply indicating whether or not she agrees with you.

2. Choose something you are not allowed to do in class now. Give reasons why it should be permitted.

Classroom Behavior Chart

Put a check mark (✓)next to appropriate behaviors. Put an (x) next to inappropriate behaviors.

BEHAVIOR	TEACHERS	STUDENTS	NEITHER
Eating and drinking	______	______	______
Talking	______	______	______
Arriving late	______	______	______
Leaving early	______	______	______
Wearing jeans and tee shirts	______	______	______
Asking questions	______	______	______
Chewing gum	______	______	______
Putting your feet on the furniture	______	______	______

Activity: **Discipline Blues**

Task: To explore different approaches to discipline

Organization: Groups, whole class

Materials: One copy of the work sheet on page 83 per student

Time: 20–30 minutes

Directions: Give each student a copy of the work sheet to complete individually. Then divide the class into groups of four and ask them to compare their answers. Ask each group to decide and tell the rest of the class what would be the most effective thing for the teacher to do.

Follow-Up: Ask the students to identify which of the sentences is

a) a threat
b) a logical statement
c) an order
d) a question
e) advice
f) a promise

Writing Output:

1. Explain what you think is the best way to maintain discipline in class.

2. Write about an incident when a teacher disciplined you. What did you do? What did the teacher do?

Discipline Work Sheet

Mrs Malloy is having a difficult time this morning in her class. The students are being very noisy and she's trying to decide what to do about it. Below are some possible things she could say. Pick out the <u>three</u> you think would be most effective and the <u>one</u> you think would be least effective.

1. If you're not quiet, you'll have to stay in at the break.
2. If we finish the lesson quickly, we'll have free time.
3. You won't understand if you don't listen.
4. Be quiet!
5. I'll tell your parents if you don't behave.
6. If I were you, I would listen very carefully to this because it will be on your next test.
7. If anyone talks, the whole class will have to stay after school.
8. You are very bad children.

Activity: **Academic Problems Questionnaire**

Task: To explore solutions to academic problems

Organization: Individuals, groups

Materials: One copy per student of the handout on page 85

Time: 30 minutes

Directions: Give each student a copy of the Academic Problems handout and ask them to answer the multiple-choice questions. Then ask them to get together in groups and compare their answers.

When they have done this, ask each group to think of a problem they have had and to brainstorm four or five possible solutions. Ask them to write their problems and possible solutions on the blackboard or large sheets of paper so that the other students can see them. After all the students have had a chance to read the problems and the groups' solutions, have them suggest additional solutions and then vote on which they think are the best solutions. Each group should keep track of the voting on their own problem.

Writing Output:

1. Summarize the results of the polling on your problem.

2. Write about a problem you've had in school and tell how you solved it.

Academic Problems

1. You are a teacher. During your class one of the students asks you a question. You are not sure about the answer. What should you do?

    a) Invent an answer
    b) Tell the student that you do not have time to answer questions.
    c) Tell the student that you do not know the answer but will find out before class tomorrow.
    d) Tell the student it is a stupid question.

2. You are a student. You have just been given a test back on which you thought you had done very well. However, your grade is poor. You believe that some of the answers that were marked wrong are really correct. You also found a mathematical error in the total number of points you got. What should you do?

    a) Tell the teacher she made a mistake.
    b) Ask another student who also knows the teacher to talk to her for you.
    c) Ask the teacher to go over the test with you and show you where you made mistakes.
    d) Tell the teacher that if she does not change your grade you will talk to the departmental chairman.

Activity: **Agree/Disagree Snowball**

Task: To examine conflicting views on the process of education

Organization: Individual, snowball

Materials: None

Time: 20–30 minutes

Directions: Ask each member of the class to draw a series of eight steps as shown below. Then dictate the following sentences:

1. Knowing how to find information is more important than memorizing it.
2. Children learn by what you do and not by what you tell them.
3. School needs to be more like real life.
4. Teachers learn from students
5. Children should be able to choose what they want to study.
6. Teachers should encourage children to express themselves.
7. In the next 50 years computers will take the place of schools.
8. The major part of education takes place at home.

Ask the students to arrange the sentences by number on the steps according to how much they agree with them.When they have done this ask them to compare their choices, first in pairs and then in small groups

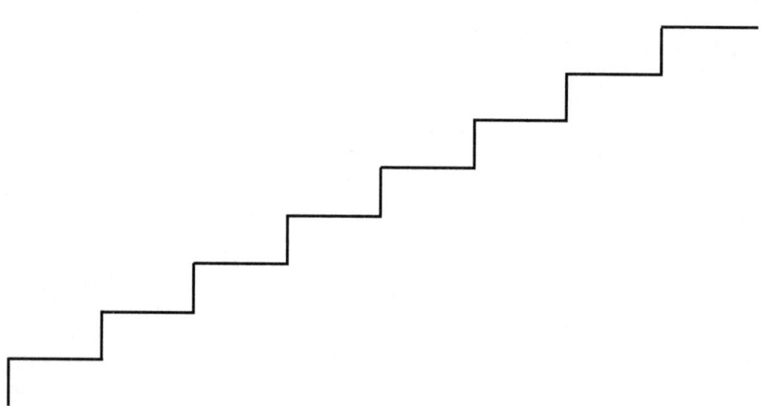

Writing Output:

1. Write about the quotation you agreed with most, explaining why you agreed with it.

2. Write about the quotation you disagreed with most, explaining why you disagreed with it.

Activity: **Edco**

Task: To explore ways in which schools could be improved

Organization: Individuals, groups

Materials: One copy per student of the handout on page 88

Time: 20 minutes

Directions: Give the students the reading passage, asking them to read it individually and to answer the questions. Then ask them, in groups of four, to brainstorm ways in which to make Edco a better place to work. Each group should appoint a secretary to report back their suggestions. If they have not already made the connection between Edco and school, ask questions to encourage them to make the link. In whole-group discussion, get them to consider the question: How could schools be improved/reorganized?

Writing Output:

1. How do you think schools could be improved?

2. Describe the perfect school.

Working for Edco

Imagine going to work for Edco. They give you a schedule that requires you to move from one room to another every hour. A bell rings every hour to tell you to move to the next place. In each room you have a different boss and are in different groups doing different tasks. You have to carry your work materials for all the tasks with you all day. You're not permitted to talk to anyone while you are working.

1. Is this how work places are usually organized?

2. Can you name any organization that is like Edco? Which? Why?

VI MEDIA: TV

1. TV Survey
2. How Does TV Affect Us?
3. Show-Time Vocabulary
4. Fear
5. Copycat Killer
6. People Appeal
7. Terrorism
8. Public Versus Private
9. TV and Elections

Activity: **TV Survey**

Task: To interview English speakers about television viewing habits

Organization: Individuals, pairs

Materials: Four copies per student of the questionnaire reproduced twice on page 92.

Time:

First lesson: 10 minutes
Second lesson: 30 minutes

Directions: Hand out the questionnaire. Tell the students that they are to find four native speakers, before the next lesson, and interview them about watching television. In the next lesson, put the students into pairs and ask them to compare the results of their surveys. After they have done this, ask them to devise some kind of chart to show the others their results. As they finish, put the charts up on the wall and ask the students to circulate and compare results.

Writing Output:

1. Write about one of the people in your survey, describing the person's TV viewing habits.

2. Describe your own TV viewing habits.

Interview About TV

Name?

Age?

Male or Female?

How long do you watch TV on weekdays?

How long do you watch TV on weekends?

What is your favorite program?

How often do you watch it?

Why do you like it?

Do you do anything else while you watch TV?
If so, what?

Name?

Age?

Male or Female?

How long do you watch TV on weekdays?

How long do you watch TV on weekends?

What is your favorite program?

How often do you watch it?

Why do you like it?

Do you do anything else while you watch TV?
If so, what?

Activity: **How Does TV Affect Us?**

Task: To sort out statements about the effects of TV

Organization: Whole class, small groups

Materials: Statements (see list below) copied on large strips of paper

Time: 30–40 minutes

Directions: Post the following statements around the room before the students arrive:

You learn about the world.
You learn about other people.
You want to buy more things.
You become lazy.
You become a better member of society.
You read less.
You believe in quick and easy solutions to problems.
You want to know more about the world around you.
You become aggressive.
You become afraid of the world around you.
You learn more English.

After they come in, explain that these are statements about the effects of watching television. Ask the students to read them all. Then have them suggest which ones they think are not true. As the suggestions are made, have the rest of the students comment on the same statements. Take down those that the majority of the students think are not true. Next, have the students individually note those which they think are positive and those that they think are negative. Have them form groups of four, compare their lists, and try to reach a consensus. Ask each group to report to the class. As they do, they should move the posted statements themselves to show their division.

After all the groups have reported, have the whole class compare their opinions.

Writing Output:

1. Choose the major benefit for you of watching television and explain why this is important to you. Give examples of specific programs you watch that help you.

2. What is the major negative effect of watching TV? Explain why it is important.

Activity: **Show-Time Vocabulary**

Task: To match vocabulary with TV shows

Organization: Whole class, groups

Materials: A copy of the Media Vocabulary List on page 95 for each student. The list may be modified to suit your students.

Time: 15–20 minutes

Directions: Brainstorm a list of 10 television shows with the whole class and write them up on the board.
Put the students in groups of four and get them to pick out which vocabulary goes with which of the shows. They should mark the shows next to the vocabulary on their individual lists. Then regroup the students so that the new groups contain at least one member from each of the original groups and have them try to agree on their choices.

Writing Output:

1. Choose a TV program that you either like or dislike and explain why you like or dislike it.

2. Write about how you think television programming could be improved.

Media Vocabulary List

entertaining	stereotyped	frightening
stupid	optimistic	honest
factual	antisocial	perceptive
attractive	exciting	adventurous
different	biased	romantic
right-wing	left-wing	one-sided
prejudiced	open	revealing
informative	intrusive	dull
normal	happy	sad
intellectual	intelligent	dumb
radical	false	canned
varied	repetitive	soap
sexy	positive	negative
hostile	mass-produced	aggressive
questioning	inquiring	factual
opinionated	stereotyped	funny
dramatic	junk	political
hypnotic	news	editorial
hyped	dynamic	

Activity: **Fear**

Task: To make supported hypotheses about a given situation.

Organization: Pairs, groups of four

Materials: A transparency of the poem on page 97, or each line of the poem, on a strip of paper

Time: One class period

Directions: Using the overhead projector, reveal the poem to the students line by line. As you reveal each line, get them to complete the designated writing task in pairs.

	I sit in my lonely room watching TV,
Stop	DESCRIBE THE ROOM
	the doors and windows locked despite the heat.
Stop	DESCRIBE THE SCENE OUTSIDE THE WINDOW
	I watch the news.
Stop	DESCRIBE WHAT IS ON THE NEWS
	A mad man is shooting people in the street.
Stop	EXPLAIN WHY HE IS DOING IT
	I switch to a movie
Stop	WHAT KIND OF MOVIE IS IT?
	and see robberies and murders.
Stop	WHAT KIND OF MOVIE IS IT?
	I am afraid to leave my room.
Stop	DESCRIBE THE PERSON

When they have finished put the pairs together to form groups of four and ask them to compare what they have written.

Writing Output:

1. Write a letter to the person.
2. Write a life history of the person
3. Explain what this poem has to do with media.

Poem

I sit in my lonely room watching TV,
the doors and windows locked despite the heat.
I watch the news. A madman
is shooting people in the street.
I switch to a movie
and see robberies, murders, rapes.
I am afraid
to leave my room.

Activity: **Copycat Killer**

Task: To examine the influence of television on social behavior and the question of responsibility

Organization: Pairs, whole class

Materials: A copy of the cut-up text on page 99 for each pair of students

Time: 30 minutes

Directions: Give the cut-up text to each pair of students and then ask them to reconstruct it. Go over the text with the whole class and then get them to consider the following questions: Is he responsible? Do the people who control television programming have a responsibility to limit what viewers can see because of incidents like this? In your country are there limits to what can be shown on TV? What are they? Do you agree with them?

Writing Output:

1. Give another example of television influencing life.

2. Write a paragraph about one kind of program or film that you think should not be shown on TV, and give reasons to support your opinion. Exchange papers with a classmate. After you have read the paper, tell the student whether or not you agree with her opinion.

Copycat Killer Text

On Tuesday, April 12th, a film was shown on television.

In the film a young man attacked and killed an old woman.

Before she died, she was beaten and tortured.

There was no apparent reason for the crime.

On the night of April 13th, an old woman was killed in the same way as the woman in the film.

When the police caught the killer, he admitted killing the woman; but he claimed he was not responsible for what he had done.

He said he was just copying what he had seen on television.

Activity:	**People Appeal**
Task:	To examine the relationship between audience, product, and appeal in advertising
Organization:	Individuals, groups
Materials:	A pile of ads for each group of students. These should be taken from a variety of magazines—e.g., women's magazines, news magazines, sports magazines, hunting/fishing magazines, and car magazines
Time:	First lesson: 30 minutes Homework Second lesson: 30 minutes

Directions:

Divide the class into groups of four and give each group a pile of advertisements. Ask them to divide them up according to who they think the advertisements are aimed at. After they have done this, ask them to go back through the piles and think about how the advertisements appeal to people. They should find two advertisements for each of the following types of appeal: sex, beauty, belonging, success, masculinity, femininity, guilt, fun, better life. Discuss any ads that don't fit into these categories.

For homework assign members of the class to watch different types of TV programs—e.g., sports, talk, sitcom, soaps, and cartoons. They should make a note of all the advertisements that occur during the show and immediately before and after. Ask them to arrange the information in the form of a chart, as follows:

TV Program	Audience	Product	Appeal

In the following lesson, the students compare their findings in groups.

Writing Output:

1. Write an account of what you found.
2. Describe your favorite ad.

Activity: **Terrorism**

Task: To explore stereotypes portrayed by the media

Organization: Individuals, pairs, small groups

Materials: Copies of the Bulletin on page 102, if students are asked to read it individually

Time: 30 minutes

Directions: Either ask the students to read the Bulletin individually or read it aloud to them. Then divide them into pairs and ask each pair to write a description of the terrorists. Put the pairs together into groups of four and ask them to compare their descriptions. When they have done this, bring the groups into a class discussion and ask them to compare descriptions again. Then encourage them to consider such questions as:

- How did they develop their descriptions?
- Did media coverage of such events influence their descriptions?
- Were students influenced by personal experiences?

Writing Output:

1. Explain why you described the terrorists as you did.
2. How is your national or ethnic group described by the media?

<u>**Bulletin**</u>

We interrupt this program to bring you the following news bulletin. Five members of a terrorist group have attacked the airport and are holding hostages. They are armed with machine guns. They claim to have bombs. They have asked for an airplane to take them to an unknown destination. The identity of the terrorists is not known at this time.

Activity:	**Public Versus Private**
Task:	To recognize and organize arguments for public or private control of the media
Organization:	Pairs, groups
Materials:	A copy of the work sheet on page 104, cut into strips for each pair of students
Time:	20–30 minutes
Directions:	Divide the class into pairs. Explain that the strips they are going to read contain arguments for and against public control of the media. Ask them to divide the strips, putting together all the arguments in favor of public control of the media and then all the arguments in favor of private control. They should then make a list of arguments for each point of view, adding any ideas of their own.
Writing Output:	1. Write a letter to a newspaper asking for more public control of what appears in the media. 2. Write a letter to a newspaper objecting to the idea of the government controlling what appears in the media.

Public-Versus-Private Work Sheet

Your TV programs in the States are too violent. Even young children can see people fighting and killing each other. In my country the government controls TV. They see to it that the programs we see are good for us.

I don't want the government to control what I see on TV. I don't trust them to know what's best for me.

Even if the government doesn't control it, someone does and that someone is large corporations. Every time you turn on the TV, you see what they want you to see.

Yes, but there are a lot of large corporations and only one government. If I don't like what one corporation wants me to watch, I can always switch channels.

Every time I turn on the TV I have to sit through endless ads. I watch TV to see the program, not the ads.

I agree, but someone has to pay for the programs. Besides when the commercials are on, I have a chance to go and get a snack.

I don't think that all that advertising is good for you. It makes you think you always need more things.

That's one way to look at it. The other way is to see that they are informing you about new products, so that you can make better decisions about spending your money.

Activity: **TV and Elections**

Task: To identify qualities that make a political candidate attractive on television

Organization: Small group, whole class

Materials: Copies of the passage on page 106, if it is used as a reading activity

Time: Two class periods

Directions: Write the words television and elections on the board and ask the students to tell how they think the two are related. Then provide them with the information in the TV and Elections passage. This can be done either as a listening or as a reading activity. Discuss the information, encouraging the students to share examples from their own experience. Then divide the class into groups of three. Tell them that they are going to invent the perfect candidate for a television campaign for president or prime minister. They should include the following information: physical characteristics, personal characteristics, and family characteristics. They may add other categories if they wish. Have each group choose a secretary to write down their lists on a large piece of paper. When they have finished, bring the whole class together and have a representative from each group present their list. The activity can be summarized by making a chart of characteristics.

Next, as homework have each group member write a paragraph about one of these sets of characteristics. The following day, have them work together to edit their paragraphs and rewrite them on a single page. Then collect the pages and pass each one out to a different group. After the students in each group have read the page, ask them to write their comments to the authors. Do they agree on the characteristics? Are there others they would include? Then return the paper to the authoring group.

Finally, discuss with the students the characteristics they have listed. Are they directly related to whether the candidate would make a good leader? What other characteristics are equally or more important? In what ways is television useful in choosing a political leader? In what ways is it not useful?

Writing Output:

1. Describe the perfect candidate.
2. Write a campaign speech or advertisement for an ideal TV candidate.

TV and Elections

Nowadays television plays an important part in political campaigns. A candidate who does not look attractive and speak well on television is at a serious disadvantage. Not only must the candidate appear well on television, but his family must, too. It is said that if Abraham Lincoln were running for president of the United States today, he probably would not win the election. He was not a very handsome man and he had an awkward style of speaking. In addition, his wife was not an attractive woman. In the 1960 presidential election in the United States, John Kennedy won a great many votes when he debated Richard Nixon on television. The voters saw Kennedy as handsome, dynamic, and young. He looked like the kind of person they wanted to have as president.